21ST CENTURY DEBATES

KT-572-702

AIR POLLUTION

OUR IMPACT ON THE PLANET

MATTHEW CHAPMAN
AND ROB BOWDEN

University of Worcester
ILS   ilding
Hen   WR2 6AJ

HODDER
Wayland

an   A1049775

School Resource
Area

A1049775

363.7392
CHA

21st Century Debates Series

Air Pollution • Endangered Species • Energy • Climate Change • Food Supply • Genetics •
Internet • Media • An Overcrowded World? • Rainforests • Surveillance •
Waste, Recycling and Reuse • Artificial Intelligence • Water Supply • World Health •
Global Debt • Terrorism • The Drugs Trade • Racism • Violence in Society •
Transport and the Environment • Tourism • New Religious Movements • Globalisation

Produced for Hodder Wayland by White-Thomson Publishing Ltd,
2/3 St Andrew's Place, Lewes, East Sussex BN7 1UP

© 2001 White-Thomson Publishing Ltd

Published in Great Britain in 2001 by Hodder Wayland, an imprint of Hodder Children's Books.
This paperback edition published in 2003

Project editor: Kelly Davis
Proofreader: David C. Sills, Proof Positive Reading Service
Series and book design: Christopher Halls, Mind's Eye Design, Lewes
Artwork: William Donohoe
Picture research: Shelley Noronha, Glass Onion Pictures

All rights reserved. No part of this publication may be reproduced, stored in a retrieval system, or
transmitted, in any form or by any means without the prior written permission of the publisher, nor be
otherwise circulated in any form of binding or cover other than that in which it is published and
without a similar condition being imposed on the subsequent purchaser.

Cataloguing in Publication Data
Chapman, Matthew
  Air pollution. - (21st century debates)
  1. Air - Pollution - Juvenile literature
  I. Title
  363.7'392
ISBN 0 7502 3877 1

Printed and bound in Italy by G. Canale & C.S.p.A., Turin

Hodder Children's Books, a division of Hodder Headline Ltd, 338 Euston Road, London NW1 3BH

Picture acknowledgements: Associated Press AP 56; Corbis 33; Ecoscene 6 (Ian Booth), 13 (Peter Currell), 37 (Eva
Miessler), 39, 51 (Chinch Gryniewicz), 41 (Erik Schaffer), 48, 59 (Bruce Harber), 52 (Sally Morgan), 53 (Anthony
Cooper); Eye Ubiquitous 11 (R. Friend), 30 (L. Fordyce); Angela Hampton Family Life Picture Library 27; Robert
Harding 9 (Ken Sherman), 34 (Occidor Ltd); Impact Photos 32 (John Arthur), 44 (Mark Henley); Popperfoto 24, 25
& cover foreground (Jason Reed); Popperfoto/Reuters 20, 26, 46, 50, 57; Still Pictures 4 (Nigel Dickinson), 7 (John
Isaac), 10, 29, 38 (Mark Edwards), 12 (Tony Crocetta), 15 (Andre Maslennikov), 16 (Mark Edwards), 17 (Roland
Seitre), 18 (G. Griffiths–Christian Aid), 19 (Arnold Newman), 28 (Hartmut Schwarzbach), 31 (Reinhard Janke), 36
(Jorgen Schytte), 55 (Tantyo Bangun), 58 (Peter Arnold), cover background (Ray Pfortner); Wayland Picture Library
23, 49. The carbon cycle (4) and the radioactive fallout from Chernobyl (43) are both adapted from diagrams in *An
Introduction to Sustainable Development* by J. Elliott, Routledge, 1999. The catalytic converter (45) is adapted from a
diagram in *Philips Concise Encyclopedia*, 1998.

Cover: foreground picture shows an Indonesian family protecting themselves from air pollution; background picture
shows a paper mill in New York State, USA.

CONTENTS

THE AIR POLLUTION DEBATE

Upsetting the balance

FACT

National air quality standards for ozone were exceeded 503 times in London during the year 2000.

The air we breathe is essential for our survival; in fact air is essential for almost all life on earth. But human actions over the last two centuries now pose a serious threat to our planet's life-giving atmosphere. Rapid population growth and industrialization have changed the balance between people and the natural environment. As we begin the twenty-first century there is a real danger that the natural systems we often take for granted will begin to fail. One such system is the atmosphere, which controls our climate and the air we breathe. According to many scientists, the atmosphere is now so polluted that we may have to face catastrophic events over the next 100 years. These events could change the way we live forever.

What is air pollution?

Air pollution is the emission of chemicals or materials into the atmosphere. Smoke from a fire, dust from a building site and gas fumes from a cooker are all forms of air pollution. Even smells and noises are types of air pollution. But not all air pollution comes from human activities. Forest fires, dust storms, decaying vegetation, volcanic eruptions and even termites have produced large quantities of air pollution for hundreds of thousands of years. In the past these pollutants have been controlled by natural cycles (e.g. the carbon cycle, opposite).

Traffic congestion is a major human source of air pollution. This is the rush hour in Manila, capital of the Philippines.

But human activities have increased the levels of air pollution so dramatically that these cycles may no longer be able to cope. Most of the air pollution produced by humans comes from power stations, factories, motor vehicles and the clearing of land for farming.

Air pollutants

The chemicals or materials that cause air pollution are known as pollutants. Some of these are obvious, like the black diesel smoke from a bus or lorry, or the white trails left by jet aircraft in the sky. However, many pollutants cannot be seen or smelt even though they may be just as damaging. Special equipment is needed to detect these pollutants so that we know when air pollution levels become dangerous. These periods are called air pollution episodes. Using modern technology, scientists are able to warn about pollution episodes in the same way as a weather forecaster warns of heavy rain.

VIEWPOINTS

'We have reached the point where we are in danger of robbing ourselves of the natural habitat on which humanity depends for survival'
Jürgen Trittin, German Environment Minister

'The Earth's climate has never been static and human impact on climate has been relatively minor compared to naturally occurring large-scale perturbations'
Nick Middleton, Geographical Magazine

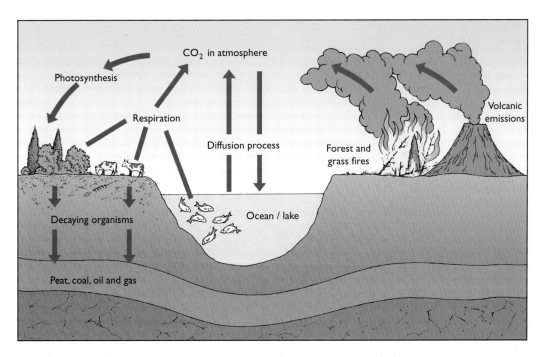

Natural systems, such as the carbon cycle, are being put under increasing pressure by human emissions.

FACT

A child born in New York, Paris or London will consume, pollute and waste more in their lifetime than fifty children born in a developing country.

Tourism could be affected as historic buildings, such as the Acropolis in Athens, are eroded by acid rain and urban air pollution.

VIEWPOINTS

'Only a few million people in China now own private cars, but that number could rise to 400 million in fifty years, as the country's population tops 1.5 billion.'
Scott Elliott, Los Alamos (N.M.) National Laboratory, USA

'Population growth is at the heart of the pollution problem as nations attempt to provide the energy, food, products, fresh water, sanitation, housing and transport needed and desired by the growing urban populations.'
Derek Elsom, Professor of Climatology, Oxford Brookes University, UK

Origins of air pollution

Human air pollution can be traced back to ancient Rome and Greece. This was when people first began to live in cities, and the high number of wood fires in a relatively small space caused poor air quality locally. However it was the greater use of coal in the Industrial Revolution in nineteenth-century Europe and North America that started the large-scale air pollution problems we face today.

Since the twentieth century, controls have been introduced to reduce air pollution. As a result, the air in industrial cities like Manchester in England, or Detroit in the USA, is much cleaner at the beginning of the twenty-first century than it was at the start of the twentieth. However, world population increased from 1.65 billion to 6 billion over the same century, placing great pressure on natural resources such as the atmosphere.

And this pressure is likely to grow, because developing countries – despite their high populations – currently account for a very small proportion of global air pollution. If these countries develop standards of living similar to Europe or North America, environmentalists warn that we will need about eight planets to support us all!

What can be done?

Despite all these problems, we *can* reduce air pollution. Scientists are continually developing new forms of energy (such as solar, wave and hydrogen power) to lessen our dependence on polluting fossil fuels like coal and oil. Technological developments have made products more efficient, and improved building techniques have made buildings less polluting.

There is also much that we can all do personally, such as walking or cycling instead of travelling in a car, or recycling bottles and cans to save the energy used in manufacturing with raw materials. Even turning off unnecessary lights could make a big difference. A good starting point is to understand more about air pollution. This book will help you do that, so that you can make your own decisions about how best to tackle the problem.

VIEWPOINT

'Children said that if they were in charge, they would do more to help the environment than adults currently do. One quarter of the children felt that the grown-ups were not taking care of the environment very well and could do much better.'
Department of the Environment. Transport and Regions (DETR) UK website

In 1990 withdrawing Iraqi troops set fire to Kuwaiti oil fields, turning the skies black with pollution for weeks. Specialist teams from the USA and Europe were sent to put out the fires.

DEBATE

Before you continue, think about the different sources of air pollution in your own everyday life. Perhaps you could list some of these sources and say what you might be able to do to reduce them.

THE POLLUTANTS

VIEWPOINTS

'Thanks to industry's long-term reliance on fossil fuels, chlorofluorocarbons (CFCs), hydrochlorofluorocarbons (HCFCs), methyl bromide and other chemicals, we are in the midst of a global atmospheric crisis that can no longer be ignored'

Jessica Vallette Revere, Friends of the Earth, in Atmosphere, Spring 2000

'Air pollution is not a modern phenomenon and not all pollutants found in air originate from human activities'

Enviroliteracy website

VIEWPOINT

'It makes economic and health sense to clean up the air in our cities as an urgent priority. Government and individuals must work together to end our love affair with the car.'

Malcolm Green, President of the British Lung Foundation

A chemical soup

The earth's atmosphere is made up of many different chemicals or 'ingredients'. These combine in differing amounts to make a giant 'chemical soup'. The main ingredients of the air we breathe are the gases nitrogen (78.09 per cent), oxygen (20.9 per cent), argon (0.93 per cent), hydrogen (0.05 per cent) and carbon dioxide (0.03 per cent), with smaller quantities of other gases, particles and water vapour.

These ingredients remain remarkably stable. But, just as adding spices to a bowl of soup will change its flavour, so any ingredients introduced into the air can change the character of our atmosphere. This is why air pollution presents a problem.

Where do pollutants come from?

At present there are lots of different types of air pollutants with new ones still being discovered and created. These can come from natural or human sources and sometimes from both. For example, methane is produced by rotting waste in man-made landfill sites, but it is also produced naturally by decomposing organic matter (such as vegetation or animal waste). This makes it difficult to tell which source is more responsible.

Many pollutants can be traced to a specific pollution source, such as car exhaust fumes or a fire. These are known as 'primary pollutants' and we can think of their source as either natural or human. Several major pollutants, however, such as ozone, are 'secondary pollutants' produced by chemical reactions in the atmosphere. Their source can be harder to trace, but because they mostly originate from primary sources we can focus on these as a priority.

Natural sources include forest fires, dust storms, swamps and decomposing organic waste. Volcanoes are a particularly important natural source – a single eruption can release enough pollutants to change the earth's atmosphere and weather patterns for several years. We cannot control these natural sources; they have always produced pollutants. Some scientists even believe that natural pollutants caused the extinction of the dinosaurs some 55 million years ago.

Human sources include exhaust fumes from vehicles, smoke from factories, and the waste gases produced by heating our homes, schools and offices. These man-made sources increased dramatically during the twentieth century, due to rapid population growth and the development of new materials and products. Many of these products led to the creation of new pollutants, such as chlorofluorocarbons (CFCs) used in fridges and aerosol sprays. However, unlike natural sources, we can control human pollution sources by changing the way we live and behave.

FACT

When Mount Pinatubo erupted in the Philippines in June 1991 it threw ash 32 kilometres into the atmosphere and caused a temporary lowering of global temperatures for more than two years.

Our dependence on fossil fuels, here being processed in the form of oil in Kentucky, USA, is blamed for many of today's environmental problems, especially global warming.

FACT

CO₂ emissions have increased by nearly 30 per cent since the beginning of the Industrial Revolution, methane concentrations have almost tripled, and nitrous oxide concentrations have risen by 15 per cent.

Monitoring air pollution

Some air pollutants are easy to identify, such as smoke which is visible or ammonia which has a very strong smell. But many, including some of the most hazardous, are invisible and have no smell. Scientists have developed special equipment to detect and monitor these pollutants. This can vary from simple detectors placed in our homes to warn of poisonous carbon monoxide to multi-million dollar satellites that observe changes in the earth's ozone layer from space. Monitoring also helps us understand where pollution comes from and how it is affected by our behaviour and lifestyles.

Installing monitoring equipment in European cities such as Copenhagen has improved our understanding of air pollution and made them healthier places to live.

To monitor all air pollutants, however, would be difficult and expensive. For this reason scientists have traditionally focused their attention on six main pollutants known to cause particular harm to people and environments. These six are sulphur dioxide, nitrogen oxides, ozone, carbon monoxide, particulate matter and lead.

FACT

US industries pump at least 1.1 billion kilograms of chemicals into the air every year.

Clean air laws have dramatically reduced certain pollutants. This gas (petrol) station in Las Vegas, USA, checks exhaust emissions and services polluting vehicles.

Traditional air pollutants

Sulphur dioxide (SO_2) is produced when we use fossil fuels, such as coal and oil. But it also occurs naturally as organic matter decomposes and when volcanoes erupt. In 1860 SO_2 emissions were around 10 million tonnes per year but by the mid-1980s this had risen dramatically to 150 million tonnes per year. Countries such as Canada, the USA, the UK and Germany were among the biggest polluters, due to their rapid industrial growth. However, since the 1980s, many developed nations have halved their SO_2 emissions. Now it is developing countries, such as China and India, which are becoming the bigger polluters.

Nitrogen oxides (NOx) are also produced by the burning of fossil fuels. Although NOx are found in nature, human activities are the main source. Internal combustion engines used in motor vehicles account for around 50 per cent of emissions, while industry contributes a further 25 per cent. Some forms of NOx can be toxic to humans, making breathing difficult and having a particularly bad effect on asthma sufferers.

VIEWPOINTS

'According to [an EPA report] emissions for all ... pollutants except nitrogen oxides declined significantly from 1970 to 1996, even though there are more people, driving more miles, and the economy is growing'
Enviroliteracy website

'Americans have made significant progress in improving our air quality and protecting public health, but challenges still remain. Too many of our citizens still breathe unhealthy air'
Carol M. Browner, Environmental Protection Agency (EPA), USA

Natural pollution sources such as this sandstorm in Mali, West Africa, turn the air so thick with particulates that you can barely see or breathe.

VIEWPOINTS

'The threat that each pollutant (or combination of pollutants) poses to our health and well-being depends on the type and concentration of the pollutants present, the length of time we are exposed to the pollutants and the state of our own health'
Derek Elsom, Professor of Climatology, Oxford Brookes University, UK

'Today's factories are cleaner by far than they were just 20 years ago, but the new pollutants are increasingly invisible. Up to 10,000 new chemicals are introduced each year with little research done into their long-term effects.'
John Vidal, Guardian

Particulate matter, such as dust, soot, smoke and other particles released into the atmosphere, is often overlooked as a pollutant. Yet it is one of the worst pollutants being generated today by factories, motor vehicles, fires, and even natural winds (as more land is cleared of vegetation, the soil can easily be picked up as dust).

These particles can be extremely small and are measured in micrometers (µm) which are a thousand times smaller than a millimetre (mm)! Particles as small as 2.5µm are regularly monitored and are known to cause severe breathing difficulties, especially for asthmatics and the elderly or young. Cities in the developing world are particularly polluted, with Cairo in Egypt recording levels up to ten times higher than those in the World Health Organization's recommended guidelines.

Newer air pollutants
New technologies have unfortunately created new pollutants such as hydrocarbons, Toxic Organic Micropollutants (TOMPs) and CFCs. These are usually produced in smaller quantities than traditional pollutants, but can be far more hazardous.

Hydrocarbons are a family of toxic air pollutants containing carbon and hydrogen used in fuels, paints, solvents and cleaning products. They are often better known as volatile organic compounds (VOCs) and polycyclic aromatic hydrocarbons (PAHs). Hydrocarbons enter the air by evaporation or when products containing them are not properly incinerated. When combined with oxygen, they can irritate the skin and eyes, make you feel sick or dizzy, and are also known to cause cancer.

TOMPs are another family of pollutants, one of the most important being PolyChlorinated Biphenyls (PCBs). Until recently, they were used in the manufacture of electrical goods and industrial fluids. If not fully destroyed by incinerators operating at over 1200°C, products containing PCBs release toxins known to cause birth defects and cancer.

FACT

In 1976 the European Community banned the use of toxic PCBs in unsealed equipment. However we are still faced with the problem of how to dispose of old or damaged equipment.

FACT

Even though global CFC production has fallen significantly, production actually rose by 87 per cent in developing countries between 1986 and 1993.

Aerosols became a symbol of air pollution in the early 1990s. The ozone-depleting propellants they used to contain are now being phased out.

CFCs were developed in the 1930s for use in solvents, coolants (e.g. fridges) and propellants (e.g. aerosol sprays). When released into the atmosphere, CFCs destroy ozone and contribute to global warming. Developed countries banned the use of CFCs in new products in 1999, but many developing countries are still using them until they can afford to develop alternatives.

DEBATE

Should we continue to develop new technologies (which may result in new pollutants) when we have not yet learnt how to control some of the traditional pollutants we produce?

INTERNATIONAL AIR POLLUTION

A global problem

Although some air pollutants are limited to their immediate environment, others affect people and places hundreds of kilometres away. Many scientists now believe these pollutants are changing the climate of the whole planet. A smaller group of scientists suggest that climate change is a natural process, and they point to the large quantities of pollutants such as carbon dioxide and sulphur dioxide produced by natural sources. However most scientists now agree there is a real danger that human actions and the air pollution they produce could severely alter our climate. The real debate is how serious these changes could be and who is responsible for them?

Trans-boundary air pollution

The air currents that produce our daily weather also carry pollutants over great distances. When pollution travels between countries like this it is known as trans-boundary air pollution because it crosses beyond the borders (or boundaries) of the country it originated in. Trans-boundary air pollution means that people and environments in far-off places are affected by pollutants that they have not produced themselves. For example, polar bears and the Inuit people who live in the Arctic have levels of chemical contamination that are among the highest in the world, even though they live thousands of kilometres from where the chemicals originate. Scientists have shown that this is because pollutants become concentrated in the blubber of the seals that both polar bears and Inuit people rely on for food.

VIEWPOINTS

'No single company or country can solve the problem of climate change.... But I hope we can make a difference...by showing what is possible through constructive action. There is no immediate crisis, and so long as we take precautionary action ... there will be no crisis in the future.'
John Browne, Chief Executive of British Petroleum, 1997

'We may have unwittingly begun a massive experiment with the system of the planet itself.'
Margaret Thatcher, British Prime Minister, 1988

Trans-boundary air pollution could be reduced if the countries involved co-operated with one another to monitor and control the pollutants. However this can be very complicated to organize. And some countries may not be as willing as others to take responsibility, particularly if they are less affected by the problem.

Acid rain

Acid rain was one of the first types of trans-boundary air pollution to be widely noticed – in the 1970s. It is formed when sulphur dioxide and nitrogen dioxide mix with water vapour in the clouds. When this falls to the ground it damages plants and animals. It has been responsible for killing entire lake ecosystems in some countries, such as Canada and Norway. It also kills trees. For example, trees in Poland have lost over half their leaves due to acid damage. And in neighbouring Germany it is predicted that 90 per cent of trees will die over the next few decades due to the effects of acid rain.

> **FACT**
>
> Around 20 per cent of forests and lakes in Scandinavia are dead and another 30 per cent have been badly affected, mostly by air pollution (acid deposition) from other countries.

These trees in Krkonose National Park, Poland, have been destroyed by acid rain. Eastern Europe has been particularly affected by this form of air pollution.

Liming helps neutralize the acid but is very expensive. It's better to reduce emissions.

> **FACT**
>
> **One molecule of CFC can result in the loss of 100,000 ozone molecules.**

> **FACT**
>
> **Human emissions of CO_2 were around 3 million tonnes at the start of the Industrial Revolution in 1751. In 1998 we emitted around 6,400 million tonnes.**

In Sweden, helicopters have been used to spread lime into acidified lakes to neutralize the acid and restore life in them. Over 5,500 lakes have been quite successfully treated in this way. But when acid rain falls on land and enters the underground water system it is much harder to control.

Acid rain also erodes buildings. In the UK alone, the Department of the Environment estimated in 1990 that it would cost up to £17 billion to repair the damage caused over the next thirty years. Many famous buildings have been affected by acid rain. These include St Paul's Cathedral in London, the Acropolis in Athens and the Taj Mahal in India.

The problem with acid rain and other trans-boundary pollution is firstly finding out who produces it and then deciding who should pay for the damage it causes. For example, most of Japan's acid rain comes from air pollution originating in China. But does this mean that China should pay for damage in Japan? In fact Japan is helping China to pay for pollution control equipment to cut its emissions, in the hope that this will reduce acid rain damage in Japan. Not all countries are so co-operative however. In the 1980s, for instance, Britain took little responsibility for its emissions across Scandinavia despite complaints from the Norwegian government.

Global warming

Perhaps the most serious type of trans-boundary air pollution is the release of greenhouse gases because this affects the whole earth. These gases include carbon dioxide, methane and nitrous oxide. They occur naturally in the atmosphere and help to keep our planet warm by trapping energy from the sun. This is what we call the greenhouse effect.

However, since the Industrial Revolution, the burning of fossil fuels and other human activities have released more of these gases into the atmosphere and upset the natural balance. In the last fifty years chlorofluorocarbons (CFCs) have added to these gases, as well as damaging the ozone layer in the stratosphere, which protects the earth from harmful ultra-violet radiation.

VIEWPOINTS

'In 1990, 49 Nobel Prize winners and 700 members of the National Academy of Sciences said there is broad agreement among scientists that the growing greenhouse effect has the potential to produce dramatic changes in the climate'
Environmental Protection Agency (EPA), USA

'The most important greenhouse gases – carbon dioxide, methane, water vapour and nitrous oxide – all occur naturally in the atmosphere, and without their greenhouse properties the Earth's average temperature would be about 33°C lower than at present'
Nick Middleton, Geographical Magazine

Meteorologists in Antarctica release special balloons to monitor the ozone hole. During the 1990s it grew bigger every year.

FACT

Australia and the UK experienced their worst flooding for fifty years during November 2000. Some commentators believe this is a sign of global warming and warn us to expect more such events around the world in future.

With more energy reaching the earth, and more greenhouse gases to trap it in our atmosphere, our planet is getting warmer. Scientists believe the earth's surface could be 2–3 °C warmer by the year 2100, causing major changes to our environment. We already appear to be seeing the results: 1997 and 1998 were the warmest years since records began. And in the polar regions large sections of ice are beginning to melt away.

Current predictions suggest that this could cause sea levels to rise by 0.5 metres by 2100. If this happens coastal areas in countries such as England, the USA, the Netherlands and Bangladesh could be seriously flooded, and some islands in the Pacific and Indian Oceans could disappear altogether. Even if we avoid large-scale flooding scientists are warning that there will be many changes to our environment and the way we live.

Greater flooding associated with climate change could lead to more regular destruction of farmland such as here in the Tana river valley, Kenya.

Agriculture could be dramatically affected. Crops such as wheat and rice may grow better in the warmer temperatures, but others – like maize and sugar cane – won't. This may lead to changes in people's diets as different crops become more suited to being grown in different parts of the world. Rainfall may become less reliable, with sudden floods and prolonged droughts seriously affecting crop growth. Irrigation can solve this problem but it tends to be expensive and wasteful. Often, less than 20 per cent of the water actually gets to the plants. On the other hand, the higher levels of carbon dioxide (which are partly responsible for global warming) are expected to increase the speed at which plants grow and so agriculture could improve. In reality we don't know exactly what will happen, but we can expect to see crop production increase in some areas and decrease in others.

Wildlife may also be affected, with certain species having to migrate or face extinction due to changes in their environment. Naturalists have already noticed that some birds are migrating later due to warmer temperatures and in Costa Rica's MonteVerde Rainforest the recent extinction of the Golden Toad is thought to be due to global warming. The ecosystems most at risk from these changes are tropical forests, coral reefs, deserts, polar regions, coastal marshes, mountains and low-lying areas.

VIEWPOINT

'...the undesirable effects of more variable weather are likely to include new stresses and nasty surprises that will overshadow any benefits'
Paul Epstein, Associate Director of the Center for Health and the Global Environment, USA

The Golden Toad may be the first of many extinctions caused by atmospheric pollution and global warming.

Warmer temperatures will also affect our health by increasing air pollution, as some cities will experience more sunshine and less rainfall, which will produce more photochemical air pollution episodes from pollutants such as ozone. This will make life very hard for people with respiratory illnesses such as asthma and bronchitis.

VIEWPOINT

'As global warming accelerates, plants and animals will come under increasing pressure to migrate and find suitable habitats. Some will just not be able to move fast enough'
Adam Markham, World Wide Fund for Nature

VIEWPOINT

'Climate change is generally considered a "northern" issue. How do you convince people with more immediate problems that they should be concerned about the gradual warming of the earth?'

Annie Brisibe, Friends of the Earth, Nigeria

FACT

Studies have shown that SO₂ pollution can travel distances of up to 2,000 kilometres in just three to five days.

This NASA image shows the largest ozone hole seen to date as a large blue area over Antarctica and the southern tip of South America.

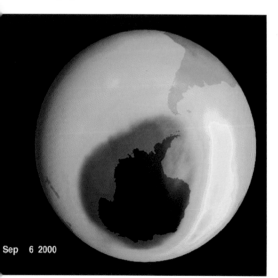

Sep 6 2000

Diseases such as malaria could increase, as mosquitoes spread over a larger area in the new warmer climates. At present, just under half the world's population lives in places where malaria exists, but scientists predict this could rise to 70 per cent by 2070. On a more positive note, warmer temperatures might reduce the number of deaths from illnesses related to cold weather such as influenza. But the harm that global warming could cause would far outweigh this benefit.

A global response?

In response to warnings about global warming, 162 nations met at the 1992 Earth Summit in Rio de Janeiro, Brazil. In the Framework Convention on Climate Change they agreed to implement national policies to reduce emissions, and share information about how best to reduce emissions without damaging economic development.

At a second meeting in Kyoto, Japan, in 1997, the same countries agreed to reduce greenhouse gas emissions to 5.2 per cent below 1990 levels by the year 2012. Some countries are trying to do more than this; for instance, the UK aims to cut emissions by 20 per cent by 2010. Such measures have been welcomed by environmentalists. But many of them say that even if bigger cuts were made immediately they would make little difference, due to the level of gases already in the atmosphere. CFCs, for example, can stay in the atmosphere for up to 100 years.

One problem is that not all countries are equally responsible for emissions. For example, on average, one American produces similar levels of CO_2 emissions to seven Chinese, twenty-four Nigerians or thirty-one Pakistanis.

Main greenhouse gases from human activities

Carbon dioxide 62%

HCHCs & HFCs 2%
Nitrous oxide 4%

CFCs 12%

Methane 20%

Source: Atmospheric Research and Information Centre

In addition, many of the poorer countries feel they need longer to reduce their emissions because of the extra cost involved in changing to newer, cleaner technologies. For this reason, European targets to reduce SO_2 emissions by 70–80 per cent by the year 2000 (from 1980 levels) were lowered to 40–50 per cent for the poorer countries of Eastern Europe.

Despite reductions in emissions, environmentalists argue that the only real solution is to start making greater use of alternative, sustainable energy sources, such as solar power and wind power.

DEBATE

Is it fair that countries producing high levels of air pollution should harm those that produce less, through effects such as acid rain or global warming? How would you persuade the more polluting countries to take greater responsibility for their actions?

World carbon dioxide emissions 1980 and 1999

Million metric tonnes of carbon equivalent

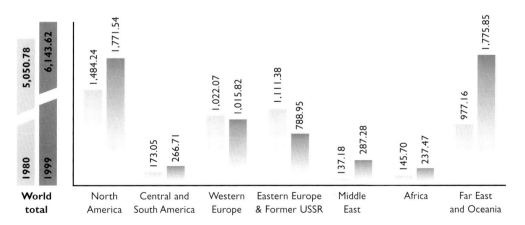

	1980	1999
World total	5,050.78	6,143.62
North America	1,484.24	1,771.54
Central and South America	173.05	266.71
Western Europe	1,022.07	1,015.82
Eastern Europe & Former USSR	1,111.38	788.95
Middle East	137.18	287.28
Africa	145.70	237.47
Far East and Oceania	977.16	1,775.85

Source: US Energy Information Administration (EIA)

NATIONAL AIR POLLUTION

A national problem?

VIEWPOINT

'There are those who are unwilling to see China progress and who are trying to contain its development by pointing their fingers at the world's environmental problems.'

China Daily, 1997

Air pollution at the national level can be easier to control than international and trans-boundary pollution, because individual countries can set and enforce their own pollution laws. In Denmark, for example, a green tax was introduced in July 1997 to encourage car owners to use more fuel-efficient cars and therefore cut down on air pollution. Those cars that use a lot of fuel are taxed more than those that can travel long distances on a little fuel.

However not all countries are prepared to take responsibility for the pollution they produce, especially if they are not greatly affected by the pollutants themselves. Poorer nations may find it difficult to pay for cleaner technologies and are often more concerned with developing their economies than with the pollution their economic growth may generate.

Who are the polluters?

The air pollution produced by individual nations varies dramatically. The biggest polluters are Japan and Australia and the industrialized nations in North America and Europe. For instance, the USA alone was responsible for around 23 per cent of global CO_2 emissions in 1998.

Poorer nations in the developing world currently produce smaller volumes of the major pollutants. At present, these nations are often more concerned about the problems of indoor smoke pollution from the burning of biomass fuels (such as wood, charcoal and animal dung). However, as their industries develop and people become wealthy enough to buy motor vehicles and other consumer goods, they will generate greater air pollution.

The fact that the richest 20 per cent of the world produces 63 per cent of CO_2 emissions, compared to just 2 per cent produced by the poorest 20 per cent, suggests that some countries are responsible for a lot more air pollution than others. However, this pattern is changing. As wealthy nations introduce pollution controls and invest in cleaner technology, the developing world's contribution to air pollution will increase. For example, in 1990 developing countries contributed 30 per cent to global CO_2 emissions but this increased to around 41 per cent in 1998, and China is now the second biggest polluter after the USA.

A Chinese petrochemical plant: China's rapid industrial growth means that it may soon become the world's biggest contributor of CO_2 emissions.

FACT

Beijing, Calcutta, Mexico City, Shanghai and Tehran were recently ranked as the five worst cities in terms of exposing children to air pollution. By breathing the air children are smoking the equivalent of two packets of cigarettes every day!

Dirty cities

More and more people around the world are living in towns and cities and their activities generate many pollutants in a relatively small area. This means that the air in our towns and cities is often full of pollutants that can damage our health and buildings. Urban air pollution is particularly bad in the developing world, in cities such as Cairo in Egypt, Mexico City in Mexico and Jakarta in Indonesia. This is partly because they use older technology that is often dirtier than modern equivalents, but can also be due to climatic conditions. Higher levels of sunlight encourage more photochemical reactions among the different pollutants, and weather patterns trap this polluted air close to the ground.

Children are especially vulnerable to air pollutants. These schoolgirls in Mexico City do what they can to protect their developing lungs.

Cities in developed countries are usually much cleaner, though they can still experience serious air pollution episodes. For example, in September 1997 Paris suffered such high levels of urban air pollution that the city authorities reduced the number of cars entering the city.

In developed countries, cities used to be much more polluted than they are today. Until the 1960s, many city-dwellers experienced high levels of SO_2 pollution due to their dependence on coal for heating their homes and producing electricity. SO_2 was one of the main pollutants in London's great smogs of 1952 and 1968 which killed around 4,700 people.

Clean Air Acts were passed in 1956 and 1968 to control the burning of coal, and many homes have since been converted to gas central heating which does not emit SO_2. As a result, SO_2 emissions from UK cities have fallen by more than 60 per cent since 1960. Most developed nations have similar policies which have made cities more pleasant and much healthier to live in.

Trafalgar Square, London, on an October mid-afternoon. Pollution from coal used in heating caused several such pollution episodes until the mid-1960s.

The problem for cities in developing countries is that they are growing very rapidly, which makes it difficult for the authorities to control their emissions. Such rapid development needs large amounts of energy and this often comes from polluting fossil fuels. In China for example, around 75 per cent of energy is produced using 'brown coal' which emits high levels of SO_2 when it is burnt. It is possible to prevent the SO_2 from entering the atmosphere, but this increases the cost of electricity production by at least 15 per cent and many poorer nations cannot afford this.

VIEWPOINTS

'Exposure to air pollution is now an almost inescapable part of urban life throughout the world'
David Calkins, ENVIRON International

'You may think you're going for a breath of fresh air when you go to the countryside, but what you're likely to get is a lungful of air more ozone-polluted than in the centre of our major cities'
Tony Bosworth, Friends of the Earth

FACT

Scientists believe that if SO_2 emissions were reduced by 30 per cent then £9.5 billion could be saved over thirty years on the cost of repairing buildings in the UK.

VIEWPOINTS

'There is widespread concern that air pollution may play a role in the induction of asthma'
1995 report by Committee on the Medical Effects of Air Pollutants in Great Britain. Department of Health

'It would be very easy for us to jump on the bandwagon and say air pollution causes asthma. But there is no evidence to back up that claim'
Anne Bradley, Director. National Asthma Campaign

Monitoring urban air pollution

Since 1974 the World Health Organization (WHO) and the United Nations Environment Programme (UNEP) have monitored urban air pollution in fifty cities across thirty-five countries. Seven main pollutants – including SO_2, CO_2, NO_2 and particulate matter – are measured and the WHO has set health guidelines for each of these so that we can protect our health.

Monitoring can help prevent illness or death such as that caused by the London smogs and similar pollution episodes in New York during the 1960s. In the last thirty years levels of air pollution have fallen to safer levels in most developed nations, but cities in developing countries such as Beijing in China and Sao Paulo in Brazil have levels above WHO guidelines and in many cities they are getting worse. In Mexico City it is estimated that air pollution is 100 times above safe levels. China is the worst country overall; it has seven of the ten most polluted cities in the world.

Santiago in Chile has been fighting a losing battle against pollution from vehicles and industry. A thick blanket of smog is an almost daily feature of the skyline.

Particulate matter

The worst air pollutant affecting cities today is particulate matter which often exceeds WHO guidelines by more than 200 per cent. Asian cities (in countries such as China, Indonesia and the Philippines) are especially affected because of their rapid increase in vehicle numbers and their limited control of industrial emissions.

FACT

In Austria, France and Switzerland it has been estimated that more than 0.5 million asthma attacks per year have been caused by air pollution from vehicles.

Asthma affects an increasing number of children and young people and there are fears that it may be linked to greater levels of air pollution.

High levels of particulate matter are known to harm people's health and in extreme cases even cause death. The tiny particles released by vehicle exhausts, industrial chimneys and domestic energy use enter people's lungs when they breathe. They can damage the lungs, making breathing difficult and leading to illnesses such as asthma, bronchitis and heart disease. Exposure over a long period can eventually lead to certain types of cancer.

In the UK particulate matter is thought to cause 10,000 deaths per year and it is known to aggravate asthma which affects an estimated 4.8 million children in the USA. In fact asthma is the main illness causing children to be absent from school in the USA. In developing countries the problems associated with particulate matter are made worse because they often lack the health facilities to treat people suffering from such illnesses.

Emissions from vehicle exhausts pose a particular risk to babies and infants, although lead-free petrol has reduced this in recent years.

National action

Governments have come up with various ways to reduce air pollution and most countries now have special departments to monitor levels and enforce laws. One such department is the Environmental Protection Agency (EPA) in the USA which was created in 1970 to monitor and enforce the Clean Air Act. The EPA has since added new laws and guidelines to further improve air quality and has been very successful in tackling certain pollutants. EPA policies to remove lead from petrol, for example, have reduced lead air pollution by 98 per cent and cut lead levels in children's blood by 75 per cent since 1970.

Many countries enforce the use of newer technology such as scrubbers, which are fitted to power stations to remove pollutants before they enter the atmosphere. Catalytic converters are another example. Combined with improved fuels (unleaded petrol, liquid petroleum gas or LPG, and city diesel), they mean that vehicles built today produce 95 per cent less pollution than those made in 1970. However the number of vehicles on the world's roads has increased by more than 260 per cent over the same period, so vehicle pollution is still a major problem.

Taxation is another way that governments can try to control air pollution, by making producers of pollution pay higher taxes than those using cleaner technologies. In Norway, for example, the government introduced a tax on older cars and paid for less efficient and more polluting vehicles to be scrapped. This resulted in 211,000 vehicles being scrapped in 1996 (compared to around

VIEWPOINTS

'Taxing a polluting activity forces polluters to take account of the effect of their actions on the rest of society'
Melinda Acutt. Economist. University of Liverpool

'Increasing the level of motoring taxation will only erode the mobility of less well-off people – particularly when public transport is so under-invested'
Automobile Association UK

Sustainable transport such as bicycles and trams (seen here in Amsterdam, Holland) can help reduce air pollution.

60,000 before the tax was introduced). In the UK new cars bought since March 2001 have been taxed according to the pollution they produce. Taxes like these help to make consumers and manufacturers more aware of their role in managing air pollution.

Some governments take a more direct role in informing the public about air pollution. For instance, city authorities in Europe can choose to hold a car-free day each September to encourage people to use public transport or walk or cycle instead of driving. In 1999, sixty-six French towns took part in car-free day and local levels of major pollutants fell by as much as 50 per cent as a result.

SO₂ emissions in Europe and North America 1980–2010 (Thousands of tonnes)

Country	1980	1985	1990	1995	2000*	2005*	2010*
Canada	4643	3692	3236	2681	2833	2914	2914
Czech Republic	2257	2277	1876	1091	462	421	376
Denmark	450	339	182	150	90	90	-
France	3338	1470	1250	958	868	770	737
Germany	7514	7732	5313	2102	1300	990	550
Italy	3757	1901	1651	1322	1004	847	842
UK	4863	3729	3731	2351	1290	1020	850
USA	23501	21074	20989	16830	15614	16250	16235
Yugoslavia	406	478	508	462	680	889	1135

NB: Germany 1980 and 1985 East and West figures combined

* predicted emissions

Source: EMEP

FACT

Urban areas, where polluting industries and traffic are most severe, are also often areas of high population. In Europe 80 per cent of the population lives in urban areas.

DEBATE

Do you think it is important to control the amounts of air pollution produced in countries, cities and towns? Why do you think some countries are not doing that much to protect their environment?

LOCAL AIR POLLUTION

FACT

Turning your heating down by 1°C, or using it for one hour less each day, could reduce your heating bills by as much as 10 per cent as well as producing fewer pollutants.

Air pollution starts at home

Even though so much attention is focused on international issues, such as global warming and acid rain, the pollutants that cause these global problems are usually a result of our own activities in our homes, schools and offices. Each time we switch on a light we use electricity which has probably caused pollution while it has been generated. Every car journey produces emissions, and even our rubbish causes air pollution as it is burnt in an incinerator or decomposes in a landfill site and emits methane gas. It is vital for all of us to understand what causes local air pollution in order to help reduce it.

Smoke from a barbecue may make the food taste good but it also adds to local pollution. Using one barbecue for many people as here, near Mount St Helens, USA, can help reduce this.

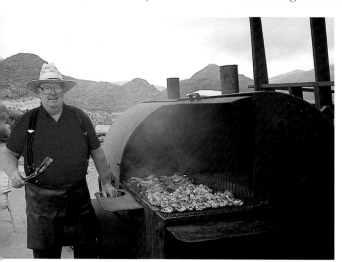

Local air pollutants

Air pollution can be very local, such as the smoke from a cigarette or a barbecue in someone's back garden. Noises, such as those made by a barking dog or a neighbour's loud music, are also types of local air pollution. Smell, like noise, is often ignored as a type of air pollutant, despite the fact that certain smells can be extremely unpleasant, making us feel sick or breathless.

Many pollutants are produced inside the buildings where we live and work and this is known as indoor air pollution. Fumes from cookers and heaters, dust and traffic exhaust blown in through open windows, chemicals from cosmetics and cleaning products, even dead skin cells from people, are all types of indoor air pollution. But some are of greater concern than others. For example, some cleaning products may contain volatile organic compounds (VOCs). These evaporate into the air, contribute to illnesses such as asthma and increase the risk of cancer. Scientists have found that VOC levels can be ten times higher inside buildings than they are in the open air.

A recent cause for concern has been the growing use of incinerators for waste disposal. As the waste is burnt, it produces toxic pollutants such as dioxins, which are known to be linked to around 7 per cent of cancers. Modern incinerators are cleaner than the old ones, but many local residents are still worried about the effect that air pollution may have on their health. In the UK, for example, experts have suggested that up to 350 deaths per year may be caused if plans go ahead to build seventy new incinerators by 2025.

VIEWPOINTS

'The older generation of incinerators have already been replaced with new, cleaner technology'
Spokesman for Department of Energy, Transport and the Regions, UK

'You don't get rid of the rubbish, you just change its nature and disperse a lot of it to the wind. It's a dangerous process.'
Vyvyan Howard, a toxicopathologist at Liverpool University

The manure being used on this German farm produces air pollutants that can be smelt by those living nearby.

FACT

Radon is the second highest cause of lung cancer deaths in the USA after smoking.

Some natural pollutants can leak into buildings through cracks and remain trapped in the still air inside. Radon is one of these and is of particular concern because it is radioactive. It can cause cancer if people are exposed to it for long periods.

Methane gas is another natural pollutant created as organic materials decompose. Methane can leak into buildings constructed on landfill sites as the rubbish rots under the ground. Special vents are normally constructed to release the methane into the atmosphere and avoid a dangerous build-up. But this does not solve the global problem because methane is also a major greenhouse gas.

Effects of indoor pollutants

We know that outdoor air pollution can be bad for our health but it is estimated that people in regions such as the USA and northern Europe spend 90 per cent of their time indoors. Scientists who study indoor air pollution have found that levels of some pollutants are often two to five times higher than they are outside. And in extreme cases they could be as much as 100 times greater. Exposure to indoor air pollutants is thought to have increased in many developed countries due to modern building methods. Double glazed windows help to keep buildings warm and save energy. But, as well as trapping heat, they also trap pollutants.

One indoor pollutant that particularly affects children's health is tobacco smoke. Second-hand smoke contains around 4,000 chemicals, including carbon monoxide,

One of the most common and harmful indoor pollutants is cigarette smoke. Breathing it in ('passive smoking') can even lead to cancer.

nicotine and tars. Many of these are hazardous to human health, affecting our breathing, irritating our eyes and causing cancer. Children breathing tobacco smoke are more likely to suffer from bronchitis and other chest infections and are at greater risk of developing asthma. In the USA alone, tobacco smoke is thought to worsen the condition of up to 1 million asthmatic children.

VOCs from cleaning products, paints or solvents can also affect our health, making our eyes, nose and lungs hurt and sometimes making us feel dizzy or sick. Many products containing VOCs now carry warnings to open windows and ensure that there is plenty of fresh air before using them.

VIEWPOINT

'As the problems of outdoor air pollution have lessened in developed countries, more attention is now being given to the problems of indoor air environments'
G.B. Leslie and F.W. Lunan.
Indoor Air Pollution: Problems
and Priorities. 1992

People working indoors with sprays need to protect themselves from pollutants.

Indoor pollutants in developing countries

In developing countries the main form of indoor air pollution is smoke from the use of biomass fuels in cooking. Wood, crop waste, charcoal, even dried animal dung are used as fuel on basic open stoves, similar to a barbecue.

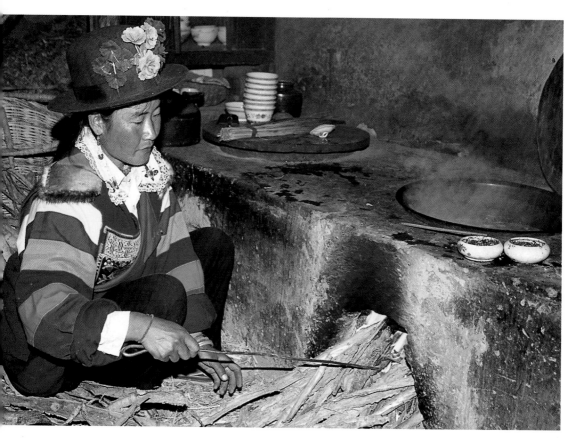

Smoke pollution from wood stoves irritates the eyes and can make breathing difficult. But for this Tu woman in Qinghai, China, there is little choice.

Used outside, the combination of many stoves can create neighbourhood pollution problems. But the greatest effects are felt when cooking is done inside, especially during the rains or in the cooler evenings. Most stoves lack chimneys or vents to remove pollutants and so they build up quickly inside the home. Women are especially affected by this because they do most of the cooking but so are young children, who spend much of their time with their mothers. Estimates suggest that 2 million people die each year due to illnesses caused by this form of air pollution. India alone recorded around 500,000 deaths per year during the 1990s. Many more suffer from poor eyesight, blindness and breathing difficulties that make it hard for them to work or study properly.

Reducing indoor air pollution

Because indoor air pollution is local there are many things we can do to reduce it. We can make sure people smoke outside, or better still try to help them give up smoking altogether. We can check the products we buy to make sure they do not have high levels of VOCs. (Many products now contain this information on their packaging to help us make these choices.) Kitchens can be fitted with extractor fans to remove air pollutants without having to let cold air – or outside pollutants – in.

Even when we have to use products that we know create indoor pollutants we can do a great deal to protect our health. For instance, it's obviously best to open the window when you are using paints or glues and wear a protective face mask if doing a dusty job such as sanding. We can also think about when we do certain jobs. For example, stripping and waxing a school floor would be best planned for a Friday after school, so that by Monday morning, when the children return, any pollutants have dispersed.

In developing countries indoor pollution can be reduced by using improved fuels such as kerosene or liquid petroleum gas (LPG) that produce less smoke than biomass fuels. Educating people to keep children away from the cooking area would reduce their exposure to the harmful effects of smoke. Fitting a flue or chimney to help carry the smoke away could also reduce pollutant levels and improve health.

VIEWPOINT

'...global ill-health from air pollution may well be dominated by the effects of indoor exposure in developing countries'
Kirk Smith, School of Public Health, University of California

In villages like this one in rural Ghana, local air pollution can reach high levels when everyone cooks their meals.

However the smoke from open fires helps to preserve the grasses used in thatched roofs and keeps mosquitoes away. If this smoke was removed or reduced it could lead to an increase in diseases such as malaria which is carried by mosquitoes.

Think globally, act locally

At the 1992 Earth Summit governments agreed to plans that would encourage people in their own neighbourhoods to become involved in local projects that would help protect the global environment. This plan is called Agenda 21 and its main message is to 'Think Globally, Act Locally'.

There are things we could all do at a local level that would help counteract international problems such as global warming or acid rain. Some of these things are very simple, such as turning lights off when they are not needed and using energy-efficient light bulbs. Others may need more planning and investment, such as improving the insulation of buildings so that they use less energy for heating.

Energy-efficient light bulbs can reduce household contributions to air pollution significantly.

Attitudes are also important. For instance, you could decide to walk or cycle short distances instead of using a vehicle. If you must use a vehicle then use public transport such as buses. A single bus carries the same number of people as around ten full cars, but takes up about a quarter of the road space.

Encouraging others to think about their local contributions to air pollution could also help. For instance, you might be able to work with your school to reduce air pollution and save energy. Even simple actions, such as sharing car journeys with friends, or better still walking, will make a difference. Don't forget that these actions can also save money and improve your health.

FACT

In heavy traffic jams, the air quality can be poorer inside the car than out. Car users regularly suffer up to three times as much pollution as pedestrians.

DEBATE

Do you think it's important to reduce indoor air pollution? How would you reduce the amounts of indoor air pollution you produce?

TECHNOLOGY AND CLEANER AIR

Cleaning the air

FACT

City diesel is a low emission type of diesel that was developed in Sweden. In comparison to normal diesel it produces less sulphur dioxide and particulate matter.

We have learnt about the many different types of air pollution we face and looked at predictions that tell us things are getting worse. However we have also seen how improved technologies have allowed us to reduce certain types of pollution considerably. New national and international targets have been set to make sure that air pollution is reduced. And higher taxes for polluters have encouraged manufacturers and consumers to think and act cleaner.

This is all very encouraging, but many environmentalists say that we are not doing enough. They argue that major changes are needed in the way we live if we are to seriously reduce air pollution from today's levels. They also argue that we cannot afford to wait any longer because, even if major changes were made today, the long-term effects of air pollution would still be felt for many years.

Many governments are building cycle tracks to encourage greater use of cycles, as in this street scene in Denmark. Similar lanes for buses often give them priority over cars.

Solar power can be especially useful in more remote areas. This panel provides power for a streetlight in Lanzarote, one of the Canary Islands off the West African coast.

Short- and long-term measures

These different approaches can be roughly split into short-term and long-term measures. Short-term measures are those that reduce levels of pollutants immediately, such as removing lead from petrol or fitting scrubbers to power station chimneys. Long-term measures aim to remove the pollutants altogether. They include the greater use of renewable energy, such as the sun to power solar cars or the wind to generate electricity, or changing our lifestyle to reduce our energy consumption. It is not always easy to make these changes, though, and many governments are concerned that making them too suddenly could cause economic problems.

Environmentalists, however, argue that the cost of adopting long-term measures is often far lower than the expense of dealing with the diseases and environmental damage caused by our current level of air pollution.

Energy demand

We all use energy in our everyday lives and in most countries this energy is generated using fossil fuels such as coal, oil and gas. We depend on these resources, even though we know they pollute our atmosphere. And our dependence has increased dramatically, with world fossil fuel usage growing by over 470 per cent between 1950 and 1998.

FACT

In the UK nearly 60 per cent of car journeys are less than 8 kilometres and 25 per cent are less than 3.2 kilometres.

VIEWPOINTS

'Emission cuts agreed at Kyoto will not be feasible without a clear application of energy-saving techniques and renewable energies in the city environment'
Alberto Mitja. Head of the Catalan Energy Institute. Spain

'I believe we already have the technology but the question is how we deploy it in the city of tomorrow'
Gustaf Landahl. Stockholm city official and co-ordinator of Zero and Low Emission Vehicles in an Urban Society (ZEUS)

FACT

In the USA wind power already provides enough electricity for 1 million Americans.

VIEWPOINTS

'Given the current economics, solar won't replace oil and gas as the prime source of energy in the lifetime of anyone in this room. Oil and gas will be required to meet the world's energy needs.'
John Browne, Chief Executive of British Petroleum, 1997

'Solar cells produce energy without emissions, even under cloudy skies. Solar electric technology will become the main energy source of the new century'
Solar Century (British solar energy company) website

Urban pollution episodes in the 1960s and the discovery of acid rain damage in the 1970s forced governments to look at ways to make energy production cleaner. Scrubbers were an early technological answer and were fitted to many coal-fired power stations to remove sulphur dioxide and nitrogen dioxide emissions before they entered the atmosphere. Modern scrubbers remove up to 95 per cent of emissions, but increase the cost of a new power station by up to 20 per cent. There is also the problem of how to dispose of the contaminated fluids used to remove the pollutants. An alternative answer adopted by several countries has been to convert power stations to use natural gas to generate electricity instead of coal. Although this is still a fossil fuel it is less polluting than coal and does not emit sulphur, which is one of the main causes of acid rain.

In the longer term, environmentalists insist that energy will have to come from renewable sources such as the sun, wind or water. This is not only because of concerns about air pollution, but also because fossil fuels are non-renewable which means that they will eventually run out. Some experts predict that this could happen within the next 150 years.

Many forms of renewable energy are available today. Although their use is still small on a global scale, some countries have made great progress. Denmark, for example, leads the world in wind power technology, with a little over 8 per cent of its electricity coming from wind farms in 1998. Danish firms are also responsible for more than half the world's exports of wind turbines and have formed partnerships with companies in countries such as Spain and India.

Solar power is also growing as the photovoltaic (PV) cells that convert the sun's energy into electricity become cheaper to make. Solar power has been the cheapest form of power for remote areas for many years. For this reason it has been used in many developing countries to power wells or provide electric light for isolated villages. Technological improvements mean that it is now possible to build roofs made of PV cells and use them to generate the energy needs of the building. Schemes to install a million such roofs by the year 2010 have been launched in the USA and parts of Europe.

Spain is among the world leaders in wind power – likely to be a major form of renewable energy in the future.

Growth in wind power over period 1980–1998

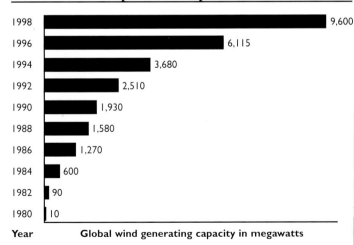

Year	Global wind generating capacity in megawatts
1998	9,600
1996	6,115
1994	3,680
1992	2,510
1990	1,930
1988	1,580
1986	1,270
1984	600
1982	90
1980	10

Source: *Worldwatch Institute Vital Signs 1999/2000*

VIEWPOINT

'Natural gas is a scarce resource and will be depleted within 60 years at present consumption rates'

Rosa Filippini, Friends of the Earth, Italy

The nuclear question

In addition to renewable energy sources, several countries have invested in nuclear power to meet their energy demands. Nuclear energy costs less than fossil fuel energy and produces none of the normal pollutants. Thus it was welcomed as a technological breakthrough in the 1950s, and by 1998 some 429 nuclear power stations were operating in countries such as Germany, France, Japan, the USA, the UK, India and China. The problem with nuclear energy is that it produces large quantities of hazardous radioactive waste which must be carefully treated and stored for up to 100,000 years.

Nuclear power normally produces few air pollutants, but one accident could have devastating effects.

Environmentalists had long criticized governments for investing in nuclear power, claiming that it was unsafe and could lead to an environmental and human disaster. Then, in 1986, an accident at the Chernobyl nuclear reactor in the former Soviet Union appeared to confirm their fears. A cloud of radioactive material was blown into the air and carried across most of western and northern Europe. Meat, milk and vegetables were contaminated, and much produce had to be thrown away. In the area around the reactor, over 5,000 square kilometres of land had to be evacuated and an estimated 10,000 people have since died due to the effects of radiation.

After Chernobyl many governments stopped building nuclear reactors, and Austria, Sweden and Italy decided to close their existing reactors.

VIEWPOINT

'I can envisage somewhere about 2050, when the greenhouse really begins to bite... people will start looking back and saying: whose fault was all this? And they will settle on the Greens and say: "if those damn people hadn't stopped us building nuclear power stations we wouldn't be in this mess." And I think it is true'
James Lovelock, environmental theorist

In some developing countries, however, nuclear energy is still in favour. New reactors are being built in India and there are plans in China to build fifty by the year 2020.

Governments have to weigh up whether the risk of accidents like Chernobyl is worth taking, compared to the damage caused by the continued use of fossil fuels. It has been proved that nuclear energy can be very clean, but a single accident could produce such catastrophic air pollution that many now believe it is not worth taking the risk.

FACT

Following the Chernobyl accident in 1986, farm animals in Denmark and Sweden were kept indoors for a whole year to avoid contamination.

Radioactive fallout from Chernobyl was carried quickly across Europe by climatic air currents.

Vehicle pollution

Motor vehicles are said to be responsible for 16 per cent of acid rain and 10 per cent of greenhouse gas emissions. Unfortunately, with over 100,000 new cars being manufactured every day, air pollution from vehicles is likely to become even worse. Although technology has reduced pollution from individual vehicles considerably over the past thirty years, the benefit is often outweighed by the overall increase in the number of vehicles. Developing countries face particular problems, as vehicles are often older or poorly maintained. Even their newer vehicles are more polluting because they use dirtier fuels and the laws controlling emissions are normally less strict.

Despite cleaner technology, growth in car sales means overall vehicle pollution is increasing in some parts of the world. In Korea car ownership has recently boomed.

As we have seen, the introduction of unleaded petrol reduced lead pollution by 98 per cent in the USA alone, and this shows that relatively small changes can sometimes have a dramatic effect. Most European countries now use unleaded petrol as standard, but in many parts of the developing world unleaded petrol is not yet available.

Catalytic converters

Catalytic converters have also reduced vehicular air pollution. These were first introduced in the 1970s in the USA and Japan and since 1993 they have been fitted to all new cars in the European Union. A catalytic converter, or CAT, is a special box fitted to the exhaust system of a vehicle. Waste gases leave the engine and pass through the CAT where platinum metals cause chemical reactions to convert them into less harmful emissions.

VIEWPOINT

'Cleaner energy sources must be put to use quickly and broadly, both in the energy-guzzling industrial world and in developing nations, which cannot be expected to cut back on their energy use'
Paul Epstein, Associate Director of the Center for Health and the Global Environment, Harvard Medical School, USA

Catalytic converters can reduce emissions of carbon monoxide, hydrocarbons and nitrogen oxides by as much as 80 per cent, but only if they reach a temperature of between 300 and 400°C. On short journeys converters do not always reach this temperature and so levels of air pollution remain similar to a vehicle without a converter.

This problem is caused by people's behaviour rather than the technology – the solution would be to walk or cycle such short distances. However, even when they work properly, catalytic converters are still a short-term measure. Carbon monoxide, for example, is turned into carbon dioxide by the converter and so adds to the problem of global warming.

FACT

The number of privately owned motor vehicles in Korea increased by an incredible 2,216 per cent between 1980 and 1996!

Exhaust gases from the engine flow through a catalytic converter. They are converted by chemical reactions into less harmful emissions.

Exhaust emissions from engine
(carbon monoxide, nitric oxide and hydrocarbons)

Catalysts (platinum/rhodium)
react with gases by oxidation

Water, CO_2 and nitrogen
emitted into air

Sustainable transport

Catalytic converters, unleaded fuel, city diesel and more efficient engines have all helped to reduce air pollution from vehicles, but they are not long-term measures. In the long term, alternative fuels must be found. Some vehicles already use alternative fuels such as electricity or solar power. The problem is that they are often expensive, slow and unable to travel over great distances without being recharged.

Hybrid vehicles, such as the Toyota Prius, offer one solution to this. The engine is part petrol and part electric, and a computer system switches between the two power sources according to the speed of the vehicle. In slow traffic the electric

> **FACT**
>
> Radiance, a Canadian solar-powered car, travelled 7,044 kilometres over thirty days using just £4 worth of electricity. This compares to over £600 worth of diesel fuel used by the support vehicle.

Hydrogen-powered vehicles like this bus in Vancouver, Canada, are seen by many as the most likely replacement for the combustion engine in today's vehicles.

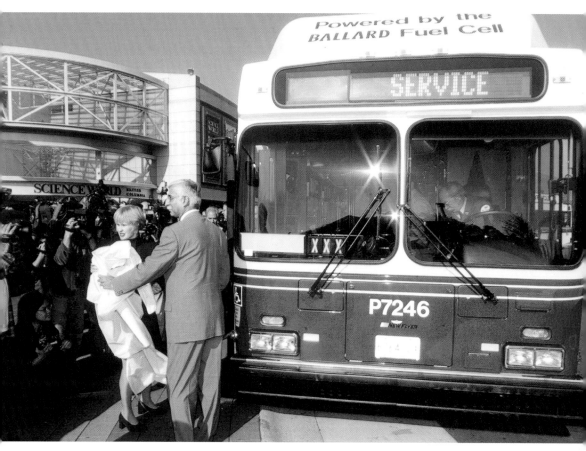

engine is used which is quiet and produces no air pollution. As the car speeds up, the petrol engine takes over as it is more efficient at higher speeds. The really clever thing about hybrid engines is that when the petrol engine is working it recharges the batteries for the electric motor so there is no need to plug it in for recharging as with earlier electric vehicles.

Forecasting technology

In recent years technology has dramatically improved our ability to measure and monitor levels of air pollution and their sources. Using sophisticated computer programs, this technology can even be used to predict air pollution episodes. Just as meteorologists can predict what the weather will be like for the next few days, scientists studying air pollution can warn if levels of pollutants are reaching dangerous levels.

This information is particularly useful to people who suffer from breathing difficulties and illnesses such as asthma and bronchitis. They are able to check their local air quality and take extra medicines, or if it is very bad they may even choose to stay indoors. Governments can also take action, as in Greece and France, where the number of vehicles allowed into major cities is reduced when high air pollution levels are expected.

Technology is not the solution

Although technology can help us to live with, and reduce, air pollution it only makes a difference if people use it. Many people resist change and this has led environmentalists to say that technology alone is not the solution. People must also change – or be made to change – their behaviour, if we seriously want to improve the situation.

VIEWPOINTS

'The rapid advancement of renewable, clean, energy sources must be THE priority for governments if we are to avert ecological catastrophe.'
Dr Jeremy Leggett. Chief Executive. Solar Century (British solar energy company)

'Simple technical fix solutions may fail to absorb the impacts of a growing population, de-vegetated land use changes, and economic growth in developing economies that are creating new sources of greenhouse gases'
Tim O'Riordan and Andrew Jordan. Centre for Social and Economic Research on the Global Environment, University of East Anglia.UK

DEBATE

Do you think technology will remove the problem of air pollution or will it just reduce the amounts we produce? Can we depend on technology alone to tackle problems such as global warming?

RESPONSIBILITY FOR AIR POLLUTION

Who will lead the way?

Cleaner technologies are often more expensive than dirty ones, and people are not always prepared to pay for them even when they understand the benefits. Electricity produced by solar cells, for example, costs up to five times more than when it is carried by pylons in a grid network. Similarly, energy-saving products such as economical washing machines or fuel-efficient cars can cost significantly more than their less efficient alternatives. Unfortunately, in a free market many consumers choose the cheaper option to save money.

Our homes could be more environmentally friendly. This eco-home in Denmark recycles water, saves energy and uses solar and wind energy to generate power.

The problem is how to encourage people to use technologies that will reduce air pollution. Governments often support consumer choice and suggest that if people demand cleaner products then manufacturers will provide them. But many environmentalists argue that this is too simple. They suggest imposing a system of taxes and incentives to make cleaner products cheaper and those that produce high levels of air pollution more expensive. In reality, we probably need to combine both approaches. The question is who will lead the way – government, manufacturers or consumers?

The Polluter Pays Principle

In recent years governments have introduced a wide range of taxes to help control air pollution and meet international emission targets. A good example is the introduction of a tax on leaded petrol in the UK. In 1988 just 1 per cent of private cars used unleaded fuel. Once taxes made leaded fuel comparatively more expensive than unleaded, this increased to 25 per cent by the end of 1989.

FACT

The Swedish tax on NOx was the main cause of a 35 per cent emissions reduction in a single year.

Even renewable sources of electricity such as the Itaipu hydroelectric dam in Brazil can produce air pollution, as rotting vegetation in the reservoir produces methane.

The idea is that the more air pollution you generate, the more you pay. This is known as the 'Polluter Pays Principle' and it is now commonly used as a basis for controlling air pollution. In Denmark, for example, a sulphur tax was introduced in 1996. This tax varies according to the level of sulphur emitted. It costs polluters US$1.13 for each kilogram of SO_2 emitted. This means that industries using high-sulphur fuels, such as coal, will have to pay more to produce their goods than those using sulphur-free energy such as wind power or natural gas.

VIEWPOINT

'It is possible to get very angry and dismayed about what we are doing to the world but it does not help. What matters is being constructive and realizing that where there is political will, much can be achieved'

Dr Topfer, former German Environment Minister

British lorry drivers protested against the cost of fuel in September 2000.

There is a limit to how much people will pay, however. In September 2000 consumers in England and Wales brought roads to a standstill to protest about the high price of petrol and diesel. This action surprised many people and was considered a warning to governments and environmentalists who might try to tax fuels such as petrol in order to help pay for a cleaner environment.

Incentives

Another way to reduce air pollution is to give incentives to individuals and companies to use cleaner methods. Incentives often take the form of subsidies, which are a bit like taxes except that they give you money rather than take it away. In Japan, a government subsidy on PV cells led to a boom in sales of solar technology, with more than 6,800 rooftop systems being installed in 1998 alone. The USA is considering a similar subsidy to reduce the cost of new solar roof systems by 15 per cent as an incentive to consumers and businesses.

A subsidy on wind power in the USA saw wind generation increase by 226 megawatts in 1998 (accounting for more than 10 per cent of the global increase that year). Germany and Spain have also introduced wind power incentives and in Spain's northern industrial region of Navarra, wind energy now provides 20 per cent of local electricity.

Warmcel insulation (recycled newspaper) sprayed into the walls of new homes can reduce energy use, and therefore pollution, considerably.

Incentives can also be offered to home owners. In the UK, for example, the government offers financial support to help people insulate their homes properly. A well-insulated home could reduce heating costs by up to 50 per cent, and because energy is used more efficiently air pollution is also reduced.

Incentives cost money

One of the problems with incentives is that someone has to pay for them. In developed countries dirty technology is often taxed to subsidize cleaner methods, but for many developing countries it's not so simple. Developing countries are usually trying to encourage new businesses; the introduction of taxes or tight pollution controls might cause people to invest elsewhere. They can rarely afford to offer subsidies either, so in many cases they have little choice but to allow companies to use the technology they choose, even if it is more polluting.

VIEWPOINT

'Taxes on motorists should be tripled to reflect the true cost of road transport, which adds 11 billion pounds a year to health bills because of exhaust pollution'
The British Lung Foundation

VIEWPOINT

'Governments should be leading the way to a fundamentally new energy direction based on clean renewable energy like wind or solar power. But at present many governments instead use taxpayers' money to support the agenda of companies which continue to spend billions of dollars on development of coal, oil gas – the climate-damaging fossil fuels.'
Greenpeace website

VIEWPOINT

'If your parents are buying new electrical appliances, like washing machines, ask them to choose the ones that use the least electricity.'
Department of the Environment Transport and Regions (DETR) UK website

Industries based in the developed world have sometimes taken advantage of this and built factories in countries where pollution controls and taxes are less strict. In this way they can make the same products for less and then import them back into their own countries to sell. However, pollution generated during the production process is suffered by people living near the factories. The consumers who benefit from cheaper goods do not normally suffer and are probably unaware of the pollution and suffering they might be supporting.

Consumer power

If consumers become aware of the pollution caused by the goods and services they purchase then they can help reduce air pollution by making different choices about what they buy and use. Consumer power can be

highly effective in encouraging manufacturers to change to cleaner production methods.

In the 1990s environmental groups were very active in making people aware of the pollution their lifestyles were causing. Their actions led to a rapid increase in demand for environmentally friendly products and gave rise to 'green consumerism'. So successful was this movement that consumers can now buy books that list 'green' products and in some towns there are shops that only sell products made by green manufacturers.

Recycling materials such as paper conserves resources, but transporting them long distances can produce numerous pollutants and may make the benefits questionable.

Many manufacturers now advertise the fact that their goods are less polluting with special symbols such as the 'Energy Star' on electrical goods made in the USA or the 'Blue Angel' on German products. Systems like these help us choose products that are less polluting, and if more people buy them other manufacturers are encouraged to join such schemes. Labelling systems are particularly effective when there is little extra cost in buying the less polluting option. For example, most Energy Star products cost little more than competing brands. And by choosing to buy these products an average American household could save US$400 on their annual energy bills.

Consumers can also reduce energy use and air pollution by recycling their waste and buying goods made of recycled materials. Recycling aluminium drink cans, for example, uses up to 95 per cent less energy and produces 95 per cent fewer greenhouse gases than making aluminium with raw materials.

FACT

If everyone in the USA bought products labelled with the Energy Star for their homes and offices over the next fifteen years then energy worth almost US$100 billion would be saved.

Most of us can recycle materials such as glass close to our homes at special collection points. Taken together, the small efforts of individuals can have a big effect over time.

VIEWPOINTS

'The economic and environmental interdependency between different countries makes international co-operation essential, since individual countries cannot tackle all natural and environmental problems on their own'

Svend Auken, Danish Minister for the Environment and Energy

'The emission targets set at Kyoto are woefully inadequate [...] The UK government has signed up to a 12.5 per cent reduction and made a pledge to cut the country's carbon dioxide emissions by 20 per cent. In fact, all these targets are inadequate.'

Dr Jeremy Leggett, Chief Executive, Solar Century (British solar energy company)

International responsibilities

Many air pollutants cause problems far from their source and these demand special forms of responsibility that might involve several countries, or in the case of issues such as global warming, the entire world. To help countries meet their responsibilities to each other, various international organizations have been established to co-ordinate policies and decide on emissions targets.

One such organization is the United Nations Economic Commission for Europe (UNECE) which was set up in the late 1970s to tackle trans-boundary air pollution such as SO_2. Under the leadership of Norway and Sweden (the countries most affected by acid rain) the '30 per cent club' was formed in 1984. This aimed to cut SO_2 emissions to 30 per cent below 1980 levels by 1993.

By April 1985, nineteeen countries had agreed to these targets, although the UK (which was one of the worst polluters) initially refused to sign the agreement. The target of 30 per cent was met by all the countries involved and in many cases they exceeded it. Austria, for example, managed to cut emissions by 82 per cent and even the UK managed a 35 per cent reduction.

The United Nations Framework Convention on Climate Change, signed at the Earth Summit in 1992 by over 160 countries, is the biggest agreement to control air pollution so far. At a second meeting in Kyoto, Japan, in 1997 the same nations committed to reducing emissions of the six main greenhouse gases by 5.2 per cent before 2012.

International co-operation does not always work, however, especially if one party is unwilling to enforce agreements. In Indonesia, for instance, farmers and companies have recently been clearing forests for agriculture and industry by burning them. Like other South-East Asian countries, Indonesia has a zero burn policy that is supposed to ban such fires, but the government has failed to enforce this law. In 1997 Indonesian fires caused air pollution that affected the health of an estimated 70 million people in Indonesia, Malaysia, Singapore, the Philippines, Brunei and Thailand. This demonstrates why countries should take their international responsibilities seriously. But it is often difficult for governments in developing countries such as Indonesia to control the actions of poor people who are just trying to earn a living.

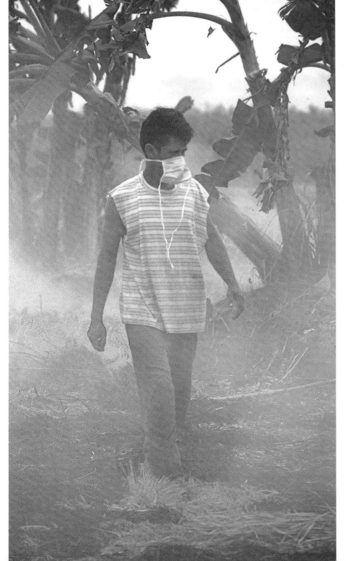

Many Indonesians have been forced by poverty and a lack of opportunities to clear forests in order to grow crops. The resulting pollution can almost turn day into night.

DEBATE

Who should take responsibility for tackling the problem of air pollution? Should it be governments, industries or ourselves, or do we all have roles to play? Who do you think should lead the way?

TOO LITTLE, TOO LATE?

The challenge ahead

As we have seen, air pollution affects us all – from local pollutants in our schools and homes to fears of climate change due to global warming and the erosion of the ozone layer. Technology and international efforts have helped reduce the problems caused by some pollutants (such as SO_2 and CFCs), but many still pose serious threats. Even now, new air pollutants are being created and scientists do not fully understand the effects they may have.

Jan Pronk, the Dutch Environment Minister, meets a protester at the United Nations Climate Conference at the Hague, November 2000. The sandbags symbolize the threat of floods due to global warming.

Because not all countries produce equal quantities of pollutants, deciding who is responsible and what should be done is very difficult. Environmentalists often complain that too much time is spent arguing over who should do what, and meanwhile the pollution is getting worse. The problem for governments is that committing themselves to reducing air pollution could increase production costs for their industries and make them less competitive in the global market. International agreements aim to overcome this problem, but many developing countries say it is unfair to expect them to meet the same targets as wealthier developed nations. India and China, for example, only agreed to cuts in CFC emissions when developed countries promised them financial help to develop alternatives.

Flooding, like this in Newport, Wales, in October 2000, is set to become a more common feature of life for many of us if climate change predictions come true.

Life on a warmer planet?

The biggest problem facing us today is the possibility of global warming. To prevent the predicted rise in global temperatures, scientists calculate that greenhouse gas emissions should be cut by 60 per cent immediately. The 1997 Kyoto agreement to reduce emissions 5.2 per cent by 2012 does not even come close to this figure.

So is global warming inevitable? According to leading experts we can now expect the atmosphere to warm by about 2.5°C by 2100 and by up to 6°C in countries such as Canada and Russia. But what will this mean for you or your children? You will probably experience more extreme weather patterns, such as heavy rains or long dry periods. You may be more at risk from diseases such as malaria or skin cancer due to greater exposure to the sun. If you live in Bangladesh, however, you could lose your home altogether. If sea levels rise as predicted, up to 6 million people in Bangladesh alone could be forced to move.

VIEWPOINTS

'You can't just say we had a flood in Mozambique and another in India and that must be down to global warming'
David Easterling, National Climate Data Center, USA

'Probably the most dramatic and visible effect of global warming in the 21st or "greenhouse" century will be the rise in sea levels.'
Nick Middleton, Geographical Magazine

VIEWPOINTS

'...many challenges remain, and there are many different views on how best to ensure that we enjoy clean and healthy air, but considerable progress has been made'
Enviroliteracy website

'We're not reducing our greenhouse gas emissions anything like fast enough to stop the effects of climate change this century [...] We can slow warming down, but we can't stop it.'
Chris Folland, Meteorological Office, UK, in New Scientist

VIEWPOINT

'...individuals can also help by changing some of their habits in quite simple ways. In combination, millions of individuals making such small changes can make a difference.'
Nick Middleton, Geographical Magazine

Is it too late?

If global warming is already happening then is it too late to do anything? Although many people may think so, it is important to consider what we *can* do. There are certain things that we cannot change, but if we were to stop trying altogether and carry on living as we do today then current carbon emissions of 6 billion tonnes could rise to as much as 20 billion in the next 100 years.

We need to solve the problems of air pollution so that people in developing regions can enjoy a better standard of living without further damaging the atmosphere. This idea is called sustainable development and this is the approach that environmentalists say we must adopt immediately. Progress can already be seen with increases in our use of renewable energy and higher rates of recycling, but there is still much to do.

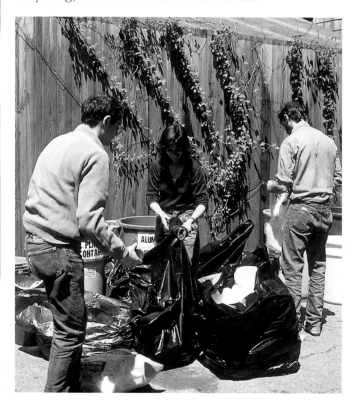

Volunteers stacking materials for recycling into plastic bags.

What can you do?

You can do a great deal to help reduce air pollution in your own life. Turning off unnecessary lights, taking a shower instead of a bath, or walking to school instead of asking for a lift could all save energy and reduce emissions. You may not think these minor changes help much, but think about the combined effect of all your friends and neighbours doing the same.

Find out about any local schemes you could join, such as this city cycle scheme in Denmark. You simply collect a cycle and then leave it at your destination.

It's also important to help your friends and family to understand the causes of air pollution and how they could reduce it. For instance, you could encourage your parents to buy low or non-polluting products, or perhaps you could start a recycling scheme at school to reduce the energy used in collecting raw materials. Many communities already have environmental programmes as part of the Agenda 21 agreements – you could find out how to get involved and maybe suggest new ideas.

You have a choice!

The most important thing to realize is that you have a choice when it comes to air pollution. This book has introduced you to some of the problems and solutions as well as the arguments about how best to move forward. There is much more you could learn. And the more information you have, the easier it will be to make choices. The main thing is not to leave those decisions to someone else – it's your future!

DEBATE

Think about all the changes that you and your family could make to reduce the amounts of air pollution you produce. Now think about how easy or difficult it would be to really make those changes. Do you think we will be able to tackle the problems of air pollution and make a cleaner future for ourselves?

GLOSSARY

acid rain this is formed when pollutants such as sulphur dioxide and nitrogen oxide mix with water vapour in the air to form an acidic solution. This solution falls to the ground as acid rain, damaging trees, lakes and buildings.

atmosphere a mixture of gases surrounding the earth, made up of nitrogen (78.09 per cent), oxygen (20.9 per cent), argon (0.93 per cent), hydrogen (0.05 per cent) and carbon dioxide (0.03 per cent), with small quantities of other gases, particles and water vapour.

biomass fuels these are natural fuels that use plant or animal waste. They include wood, crop stalks, animal dung and collected leaves. They are normally dried and burnt, but animal dung can be used to produce a type of gas called biogas.

catalytic converter a filter fitted to a car exhaust to reduce harmful emissions such as carbon monoxide and nitric oxides. They are converted into less immediately harmful carbon dioxide, nitrogen and water.

CFCs the abbreviation for a group of chemicals called Chloro-Fluoro-Carbons that destroy ozone in the atmosphere for up to 100 years after they are released.

They have been used in refrigerators, fire extinguishers and some aerosol sprays. Today their use is banned in new products.

developed countries the wealthier countries of the world, including Europe, North America, Japan, Australia and New Zealand.

developing countries the poorer countries of the world, sometimes called the Third World, and including most of Africa, Asia, Latin America and Oceania.

dioxins highly toxic chemical wastes produced during the manufacture or disposal of products such as electrical goods and herbicides for controlling weeds. Dioxins can also be produced when incinerators do not fully burn plastic waste.

ecosystem the contents of an environment, including all the plants and animals that live there. This could be a garden pond, a forest, or the whole of planet earth.

emissions waste products (normally gases and solid particles) released into the atmosphere. These include car exhaust fumes and the wastes from chimneys at power stations and factories.

fossil fuels energy sources such as coal, oil and gas formed millions of years ago by the fossilized remains of plants and animals.

global warming the gradual warming of the earth's atmosphere as a result of greenhouse gases trapping heat. Human activity has increased the level of greenhouse gases, such as carbon dioxide and methane, in the atmosphere.

greenhouse gas an atmospheric gas that traps some of the heat radiating from the earth's surface.

hydrocarbons a family of toxic air pollutants containing hydrogen and carbon that are released by fossil fuels and used in fuels, paints, solvents and cleaning products. They include VOCs and PAHs (see separate Glossary entries).

methane a greenhouse gas produced by decomposing organic matter such as rotting vegetation or landfill sites. It is also a by-product of the digestive system of cows and of rice cultivation.

organic a product of living organisms that occurs naturally in the environment. Organic substances can be broken down by nature – they are biodegradable.

ozone there are two types of ozone, stratospheric and tropospheric ozone. Stratospheric ozone is found in the upper atmosphere and protects us from the sun's harmful ultra-violet rays. Tropospheric ozone is a pollutant made when sunlight, hydrocarbons and nitrogen oxides react together in the lower atmosphere.

PAHs the abbreviation for a class of air pollutants called Polycyclic Aromatic Hydrocarbons which are emitted from vehicle exhausts.

particulate matter a type of air pollution that is made up of very small particles such as dust, soot and smoke.

PCBs the abbreviation for a group of chemicals called Poly-Chlorinated Biphenyls used in electrical goods and some plastics. PCBs release dioxins if not properly disposed of in incinerators at over 1200°C.

PV cells the abbreviation for Photo Voltaic cells which convert the sun's energy into an electric current. They are used to provide power for electrical goods (calculators, watches, etc), buildings and even the new international space station.

renewable energy sources energy sources that are easily replaced or replace themselves, to be used again (e.g. sun, wind and water, used for solar, wind and wave power). Fossil fuels are not renewable because they take millions of years to replace themselves.

scrubbers filters attached to chimney stacks to remove harmful gases by absorbing them in a liquid. In coal-fired power stations they are used to remove sulphur dioxide and reduce acid rain.

slurry a liquid containing a large quantity of solid material, normally like a thick paste. Farmyard slurry is diluted animal waste.

TOMPs the abbreviation for Toxic Organic Micro Pollutants. A group of pollutants produced by the incomplete burning of fuels or waste. They are highly toxic, even in small quantities, and some are carcinogenic. PCBs are one of the most important pollutants in this group.

VOCs the abbreviation for Volatile Organic Compounds. A group of pollutants emitted by vehicle exhausts and products such as paints and solvents.

BOOKS TO READ

A Green World? (Viewpoints series)
Nicola Baird (Franklin Watts, 2001)

Just the Facts: Global Pollution
Adrian Cooper, Rob Bowden and
Richard Bingley (Heinemann, 2002)

Air Alert: Rescuing the Earth's Atmosphere
Christina Miller and Louise Berry
(Atheneum Books, 1996)

Protecting Our Planet: Keeping the Air Clean
John Baines (Hodder Wayland, 2000)

USEFUL ADDRESSES

http://www.epa.gov/students
The student pages of the United States Environmental Protection Agency provide information, facts and data on environmental issues including air pollution.

http://www.georesources.co.uk
This site allows you to select geography and environment study topics by category and age group and then provides links to the most useful internet sites.

http://www.enviroliteracy.org
A very good educational site searchable by topic and including air as a key category. Provides its own information files with direct links to information on other topical sites.

http://www.greenpeace.org
The website for the environmental action group Greenpeace. Contains news and information about current and past debates as well as useful links to other organizations.

http://www.foe.org
The US site for Friends of the Earth provides information about current environmental campaigns as well as links to other useful sites.

http://www.foe.org.uk
The UK site for Friends of the Earth provides information about current environmental campaigns as well as links to other useful sites.

http://www.defra.gov.uk/environment/
climatechange/schools/index.htm
This site, provided by the UK government, has a wealth of information on global warming. Includes facts, activities, quizzes and links to other sites.

http://www.ace.mmu.ac.uk
The Atmospheric Research and Information Centre at Manchester Metropolitan University has lots of useful information on air pollution. This site includes an on-line encyclopedia, fact sheets, study packs and a newsletter to keep you up to date with air pollution issues in the UK, Europe and around the world.

Council for Environmental Education
94 London Street
Reading
RG1 4SJ
Tel: 0118 950 2550

Friends of the Earth
26–28 Underwood Street
London N1 7JQ
Tel: 0207 490 1555

Greenpeace
Canonbury Villas
London N1 2PN
Tel: 0207 865 8100

Greenwatch Ltd
6 Addison Avenue
London W11 4QR
Tel: 0207 603 6731

World Resource Foundation
Heath House
133 High Street
Tonbridge
Kent TN9 1DH
Tel: 01732 368333

INDEX